THREE FRESHWATER FRIENDS

TENNYSON, WATTS
AND
MRS. CAMERON

by

HESTER THACKERAY FULLER

FOREWORD BY HER NIECE
Belinda Thackeray Norman-Butler

EDITOR
Elizabeth Hutchings

PHOTOGRAPHS

Front Cover .... *Freshwater Bay with Tennyson Down 1989*
Richard J Hutchings

Page 6 .... *Tennyson at Compton*
Elizabeth Hutchings

Page 10 .... *Alfred, Lord Tennyson*
Julia Margaret Cameron

Page 22 .... *G.F. Watts, O.M., R.A.*
Julia Margaret Cameron 1892

Page 30 .... *Mrs. Julia Margaret Cameron*
Henry Herschel Hay Cameron,
One of Mrs. Cameron's sons, signed and dated 1870.

In the collection of the Royal Photographic Society. Featured in
Julia Margaret Cameron – Her Life and Photographic Work
By Helmut Gernsheim. Pub. 1948

© E. Hutchings and B. T. Norman-Butler

ISBN 0 9504736 8 5

1st	Edition 1933	Isle of Wight County Press
2nd	Edition 1936	Isle of Wight County Press
3rd	Edition 1992	Hunnyhill Publications
4th	Edition 1993	Hunnyhill Publications
	Reprint 1996	Hunnyhill Publications

Published by Hunnyhill Publications
Corner Cottage, Hunnyhill, Brighstone, Newport, Isle of Wight. PO30 4DU
Tel: (01983) 740363

Printed by Biltmore Printers
Cross Street, Newport, Isle of Wight. PO30 1PT

FOREWORD

Three Freshwater Friends was written by my Aunt Hester, who after her father died dedicated her life to her Mother, Anne Thackeray Ritchie. Hester was so steeped in the memories and affections of the past that she has enabled us to see the Poet, the Painter and the Photographer striding along High Down, reading aloud under the evening trees or developing films in a dark cupboard, as her Mother saw them.

The link between Tennyson and Thackeray was forged in 1827 when the young Alfred and the young William went up to Trinity College Cambridge and joined a fraternity of genius. Hallam was Tennyson's beloved friend while Fitzgerald became Thackeray's favourite companion but there were many others in this group who laughed and argued together as happily as undergraduates do today.

Tennyson and Thackeray shared a great deal in common as their lives progressed. Both endured and survived long years of frustration, sorrow and poverty. Tennyson's Father became insane and Thackeray's wife lost her reason, through the strain of childbirth. At this time of stress the Bank of Bengal collapsed leaving him with an incapacitated wife and two small daughters to provide for. He was forced to send the girls to live with his Mother in Paris while he became a "penny-a-liner in grub street," literally writing reviews, essays and articles for dear life. Ten years were to pass before he could establish a home for his beloved Anny and Minny and also have enough ready money to concentrate on writing Vanity Fair.

This great novel brought him fame. The children brought him happiness. It was very unusual in those days for a Father to take endless trouble in the upbringing of ten and twelve year old girls. He introduced them to all his friends who responded with great generosity. Anny and Minny were invited to Little Holland House to share in the Princeps' adulation of Watts and the eccentric kindness of Mrs. Cameron. They dropped Mrs. Carlyle's medicine on her counterpane but were welcomed nonetheless. They played charades with the Dickens family and listened with amusement to Miss Brontë's dreary conversation at dinner. They enjoyed the sight of dusky Tennyson, elegant D'Orsay and faithful Fitzgerald who often came to visit their Father.

G. F. Watts painted Anny's portrait, head and shoulders only, in 1859. A few months later, her first novel, *The Story of Elizabeth* came out and was well reviewed so 'Signor', as all his friends called Watts, added an extra 4 inches to the length on which he painted her hands holding a book with a white rose lying on the open page.

Anny asked Signor whether he would paint a posthumous picture of her father for Trinity College, Cambridge – 'I am grieved', he wrote, 'that I cannot do what you wish. I would have given much to paint him and asked him to sit for me more than once. I should be sure to fail. My memory for faces and characteristics is curiously bad.'

The only shadow on Anny's and Minny's happiness was anxiety about their Father's health. He died suddenly on Christmas Eve 1863, leaving two distraught unmarried young women in their early twenties. Alfred and Emily Tennyson travelled up to London immediately to share and assuage their grief.

Mrs. Cameron had recently moved to Freshwater Bay and bought two adjoining cottages from Mr. Long. She had built a tower to unite them and called the whole Dimbola after her husband's coffee estates in Ceylon. Early in the new year she lent one side of the house to Anny and Minny. On arrival the girls became aware of a dark figure gazing in at the window. It was Tennyson come to see if all was well. They depended more and more on his down-to-earth good sense and brilliant conversation, while Mrs. Cameron's amazing achievements and enthusiastic absurdities invigorated their spirits.

She was the ugly duckling in a clutch of beautiful Pattles and had more drive and personality than any of them. She not only mastered the art of photographic portraiture but she took up other causes with equal zest. On one occasion she imported a doctor to vaccinate her immediate entourage. Having cornered everyone at Dimbola she marched up to Farringford. Warned of her intent the Poet bolted up the back stairs and locked himself into his study. She pursued him and was heard hammering at the door shouting, "Come out Alfred, you coward." And out he came to be vaccinated.

When Minny married Leslie Stephen in 1867 Watts' present was her portrait. Anny went to live with the young couple and Minny made her two authors very comfortable indeed. They were therefore all the more devastated when she died in childbirth. Signor painted a copy of Minny's portrait to comfort Anny. Two years later she married her much younger cousin Richmond Thackeray Ritchie and had two children, Hester and William. Alfred Tennyson stood godfather to William and Anny became godmother to the poet's grandson Charles Tennyson. He used to laugh when he told stories of her charm and fun.

Anny visited Signor at Limnerslease just before he died in 1904. He told her, 'As long as I can work and improve I care to live.' He was sculpting the equestrian group for the Cecil Rhodes Memorial which he called, *The man looking out on Rhodes' unfinished work.*

In 1907 Hester took a lease on the Porch, (a cottage which Mrs. Cameron had built in The Square, opposite Dimbola), in order to have a permanent base in Freshwater. Her Father, now Permanent

Under Secretary for India was immensely busy in Whitehall and needed rest and recreation, while William's growing family, James, Belinda, Catherine and Maisie enjoyed marvellous holidays with donkey carts and picnics, which are well recorded in our family photograph albums.

Sir Richmond Ritchie died of 'flu and overwork in 1912. His wife and daughter spent more and more time at The Porch, (one of the very few local houses to be bombed during the Second World war and never rebuilt). The Porch provided Lady Ritchie with the title of her last book. Grandmama, as we called her fell ill early in 1919. Hallam Tennyson called every day to see his old friend and bid farewell. As a last gesture of affection he draped her coffin on its way to London with the beautiful pall which was embroidered for his Father, the Poet Laureate's last journey to Westminster Abbey. It is now exhibited at Carisbrooke Castle with the Poet's hat and cloak.

Hester sold her Chelsea house and The Porch and bought Pannells which faces south between Terrace House and Redoubt House next to Dimbola. She edited her Mother's letters and collaborated in a charming memoir entitled *Thackeray's Daughter*.

Hallam's second wife, May, Lady Tennyson and Hester became devoted friends. They raised money for the West Wight Ambulance and planned a lending library. To this end Lady Tennyson bought the then rather ugly house at the foot of Afton Down beside old Mr. Cotton's boat house. Every morning she set off in a fly to pick up Hester and spend the day with her sorting books and eating bananas like school girls! They were helped in their task by Lady Tennyson's librarian, Allan May.

Lord and Lady Tennyson were endlessly good to the four Ritchie children. We called them Alum Bay, (Hallam's joke) and Maida-in-the-Moon, (which was her style.) The Tennyson boys became our great friends. Penrose and Julian Tennyson and our brother James all fell in the second great war.

Lord Tennyson relied on Hester to entertain the many visitors who came to see Farringford. On one occasion a Bostonian couple Mr. and Mrs. Richard Fuller were so entranced with their dark-eyed, impulsive hostess that they called on her next day. A pen-friendship ensued and when Mrs. Fuller died the widower was much comforted by Hester's letters. A year later he came in person and persuaded her to marry him.

They were very happy and it was Uncle Richard who published Three Freshwater Friends. After his death Hester left Freshwater to live next door to her brother and sister-in-law. Apart from her self-imposed valedictory task Hester was a gifted gardener with a brilliant colour sense and a talent for finding unusual prints and ornaments. Nowadays she would have had a career as a garden designer or an interior decorator, but in her generation few women on their own broke away from the family net-work.

It would have been happier for her if she had not devoted herself entirely to the past, but in that case we should not have the pleasure of reading Three Freshwater Friends as republished in Tennyson's Centenary Year, followed by this revised edition.

Belinda Thackeray Norman-Butler 1993

PUBLISHERS' NOTE

The publishers are indebted to Mrs. Jean Flynn of the Julia Margaret Cameron Gallery, High Street, Cowes for identifying the three original photographs.

**ALFRED LORD TENNYSON
WITH KARÉNINA**

THE LAUREATE'S LINCOLN STATUE

When Lord Brownlow, Lord Lieutenant of Lincoln mentioned the proposal to erect a statue to commemorate the life of this man born at Somersby Rectory in the Lincoln Wolds the 80 year old Watts asked if he might undertake the work for nothing as a tribute to his friend. This was a typical gesture from a magnanimous old man who, if it had been practical would always have created his art for nothing.

Watts was still working in London on his huge equestrian statue, which had returned from the foundry after being cast for the Cecil Rhodes Memorial. He had seen this bronze in the courtyard of Burlington House and not been satisfied with it. As *Physical Energy* the second casting now stands in the centre of Kensington Gardens. In spite of this he set about the task of sculpting Tennyson, though with no great alacrity. The first figure seems to have fallen down and there had to be a restart.

When he wanted details of how to carve the dog which shelters under his master's great cloak, looking up at him, perhaps in expectation of a walk on High Down above Farringford, he wrote to Briton Riviere, who had painted a portrait of Audrey, the second Lady Tennyson. It is entitled *Lady Tennyson and the Poet's Old Wolfhound, Karénina*. Its whereabouts now seems a mystery .*

Watts wrote, "Please tell me what was the breed of dog that

---

* *Someone reading this may know the answer and could inform the publishers for inclusion in future editions. Lady Tennyson is on a mossy, flowery bank with her arm round Karénina.*

you painted with Lady Tennyson and the proportion of the breadth of the chest to the length of the head; also, what sort of tail; if you would sketch the forepaws and the hind; I should be more indebted than I can say."

Ten months before his death Watts was saddened when the day came for the men from Singers' Foundry at Frome in Somerset to put the great statue on a canvas stretcher and load it onto a waggon for its slow and careful cross-country journey. In her *Annals of an Artist's Life* his widow, Mary writes, "Signor saw it going with real suffering: 'I think what it might have been,' he said." Like all true artists he was never satisfied with his work but when the bronze was unveiled outside Lincoln Cathedral on July 15, 1905 all were pleased. The subject is *The Flower in the Crannied Wall*, not as some wags say *The Disappointed Cabbie!* If you look carefully at the bronze you can see the long sprig of ivy-leaved toadflax hanging from his left hand. Christopher Turnor took a photograph of the sculptor in August 1903 working on the statue up to the last minute before its long journey, never to see it again.

Now Poet, Horse and Rider can be seen at the Watts Gallery and it is well worth a visit. The foundation stone was laid by Watts on 23 February 1903, Watts' 86th birthday, and he lived just long enough to perform the opening ceremony in 1904. It was not only to house many of his paintings but part of it was to be used as a hostel for young men who came to work in Mary Watts' pottery. There is now a resident curator, Richard Jefferies who, with his assistant Hilary Morgan makes everyone welcome. Between them they have a prodigious fund of knowledge and information to impart about anything whatsoever to do with Signor, that grand old man.

Elizabeth Hutchings 1993

ALFRED LORD TENNYSON

To us who live at Freshwater every stone, has significance, every green lane and path association. Great men cast a benediction upon the places where they have lived, and Freshwater is hallowed ground as having been the home of Alfred Lord Tennyson and for a short time of George Frederick Watts, O.M., R.A.

Memories quickly pass away, changes arrive with such unexpected and diabolic force that tradition vanishes, and the aim of this little guide has been to try to recall the past, and introduce those who come to the Freshwater of to-day to the Freshwater that Tennyson knew and loved and which, for all time, holds a very remarkable place in literary history.

The life at Freshwater in the days of which I write was peculiar to the place, for though it was completely out of the world it was at the same time, owing to Tennyson, in close touch with all that was new and most interesting in literature and science.

The Isle of Wight was then so remote and far away that a porter at Yarmouth would call out for the benefit of departing travellers: "This way for England." The steamer came and went from the quay behind the Yarmouth Pier Hotel, and the journey to Freshwater was made by a coach drawn by two horses. These were the days when we would think nothing of walking from the steamer to Freshwater, following the footpath across the fields past the old Church built by William Fitz-Osborne in the thirteenth century and given by him to the monks of Lyra in Normandy, and from thence to the Bay, where

ALFRED, LORD TENNYSON

" All things through thee take nobler form,
And look beyond the earth."

our pilgrimage into the past shall begin by going at once to Farringford, the home of Tennyson. As we make our way along the quiet road the following words of Henry Cameron* seem appropriate to quote, for they sum up the feeling of love that we who belong to the Past have for the place: "Dear Farringford ! Not only is it supremely beautiful in itself but it is full of the tenderest recollections for me of a sunny boyhood. *Ille terrarum mihi praeter omnes angulus ridet.* I see once more the stately figure of the Poet slowly moving along the grass path in the shadow of the overhanging boughs. And, up the path leading to 'the ridge of the noble down,' I see again that company of friends, each one in turn, as they visited the Farringford Poet: astronomer, painter, sculptor, actor, scholar, and divine."

Farringford was Tennyson's home for thirty-nine years. The story is well known of how the Poet and his wife one November evening rowed across the Solent in an open boat and "one dark heron flew over the sea, backed by a daffodil sky." They came to Farringford and found there all the loveliness and beauty they had been looking for since they first married. The glorious view of Afton Down from the drawing room windows and the lovely glimpses of the English Channel through the elms and chestnut trees, made them decide that they had come to the ideal place in which to live. The trees have grown higher and thicker, a few have lately been cut down, but except for that Farringford remains practically as it was eighty years ago when the Poet first came.

The house was taken on trial in 1853, and then three years later it was purchased, and Lady Tennyson wrote to her friend and neighbour Mrs. Cameron: "The ivied house amongst the pine trees is ours," and ever since that day Farringford has been the home of the Tennyson family. **

* *The son of Mrs. Cameron, he passed his boyhood at Dimbola, Freshwater Bay.*
** *Farringford was sold in the 1950's (Ed. 1993)*

Lady Tennyson writes to the same friend of the new house: "It is tantalising to have a big, smooth, rounded down just in front of a large window, and to be forbidden by the bitter winter blasts to climb it. It is a pity the golden furze is not in bloom, for when it is it makes a gorgeous contrast to the blue sea . . . . Alfred has been reading Hamlet to me, and since then has been down to the Bay by the loud voice of the sea. There is something so wholesome in beauty, and it is not for me to try to tell of all we have here in those delicate tints of a distant Bay and the still more distant headlands. These I see every day with my own eyes and so many with his, when he comes back from his walk." The closing sentence about eyes makes me think of Rudyard Kipling's advice to me. "Use your eyes," he said. "No one knows what they lose from not looking."

Walks were the custom at Farringford, and the Poet would go out each day with a friend, whatever the weather, along the Down Lane and then up to High Down, now called Tennyson Down, of which he wrote to F. D. Maurice, inviting him to stay: "The air is worth as somebody said 'sixpence a pint.' " My mother, Lady Ritchie, the eldest daughter of W. M. Thackeray, in her Essay on Tennyson, says: "Walked with Tennyson along High Down listening to his talk, while gulls came sideways flashing their white breasts against the edge of the cliff, and the Poet's cloak flapped time to the gusts of the west wind." Of the home she writes: "The house at Farringford itself seemed like a charmed palace, with green walls without and speaking walls within. There hung Dante with his solemn nose and wreath. Italy gleamed over the doorways, friends' faces lined the passages, * books filled the shelves, and a glow of crimson was everywhere. The oriel drawing-room window was full of green and golden leaves and the sound of birds and the distant sea."

Photographic portraits by Mrs. Cameron.

Bayard Taylor, in his Autobiography, gives an account of a walk with Tennyson, who he describes as "a man tall and broad-shouldered as a son of Anak, with hair, beard, and eyes of southern darkness."

"We climbed the steep coomb of the chalk cliff and slowly wandered westward till we reached the Needles. During the conversation with which we beguiled the way, I was struck with the variety of the Poet's knowledge; not a little flower on the Down which the sheep had spared escaped his notice, and the geology of the coast, both terrestrial and submarine, was perfectly familiar to him."

Tennyson studied the geology of the Isle of Wight with enthusiasm, and Allingham, the friend of Tennyson, has recorded in his published diary the following scrap of geological talk. It was a summer evening at Farringford; they were sitting after dinner in the drawing-room and Tennyson spoke of boys catching butterflies. He said: "Why cut short the butterflies' lives ? What are we ? We ourselves are the merest moths. Look at that hill (pointing to Afton Down through the large window in the drawing-room), it is four hundred million years old. Think of that ! Let the moths have their little lives."

II

Freshwater in the days of Tennyson has been compared to Athens in the time of Pericles, as being the place to which all the famous men of the reign of Queen Victoria gravitated. They came to Freshwater on a pilgrimage and to Farringford as if to a shrine. To quote from a contemporary writer: "They worshipped Alfred Tennyson as the well-head of an enchanting river of song; the charm of his personality and the beauty of his surroundings at Farringford came in addition to make a precious setting for the jewel of his genius."

Tennyson's word was law, and his poetry the inspiration of thousands. These days are so far away from us now that it is a little difficult to communicate to present-day readers the power of the Poet's influence, not only upon his personal friends, but upon the public, who only knew him through his books. By his friends he was known by the name of King Alfred, no name less than king seeming adequate to sum up his genius and express his bigness of heart. The Poet was consulted by the public on every imaginable subject, from a clergyman who had lost his faith, to a father who wanted a name for his new-born child.

An illustration of Tennyson's influence is given in Mr. Allingham's published Diary, where the story is told in the Poet's own words. "I was staying at an hotel in Covent Garden and went out one morning for a walk. A man met me, tolerably well dressed, but battered looking. I had never seen him before. He pulled off his hat and said, 'Beg pardon, Mr. Tennyson, might I say a word to you?' I stopped. ' I've been drunk for three days and I want to make a solemn promise, Mr. Tennyson, that I will drink no more.' I said that was a good resolve and that I hoped he would keep it. 'I promise you that I will, Mr. Tennyson,' and he added, 'Might I shake your hand?' I shook hands with him, and he thanked me and went on his way.

Hallam Lord Tennyson once told me he was walking with his father and a stranger touched him on the arm and said, "Do you know who it is with whom you are walking ?" Hallam Tennyson replied, "Yes my father." "Nonsense, man," answered the stranger. "You are walking with the Poet Tennyson." Nathaniel Hawthorne records of Tennyson, "I liked him well and rejoiced more in looking at him than in all the wonder of the Exhibition." (The Great Exhibition of 1851).

No wonder the Poet built the bridge over Tennyson Lane to escape from his admirers. It still stands as he made it, so that by crossing over the bridge, he could avoid the crowds who would gather at the green door in the lane, on the chance of seeing the Poet come out for his daily walk. After hours of waiting all that could be seen by the public was a flash of the Poet's cloak and hat, as, with bent head, he raced across the bridge from his garden into "The Wilderness" and from thence on to the Down.

What he looked like we know from Carlyle's word portrait of him: "One of the finest-looking men in the world. A great shock of rough, dusky, dark hair; bright, laughing hazel eyes; massive, aquiline face, most massive yet most delicate; of sallow, brown complexion, almost Indian looking; clothes cynically loose, free, and easy; smokes infinite tobacco; his voice is musical, metallic, fit for laughter and piercing wail, and all that may lie between; speech and speculation free and plenteous; I do not meet in these last decades such company over a pipe."

An old friend of my family and the Tennysons has written of the Poet's talk and says: "It was far and away the most enjoyable I have ever listened to, with its dry humour shading off suddenly into vehement earnestness, its felicity of epithet that at times flashed out like a searchlight and lighted up the whole subject of discussion, its underlying vein of robust common sense and its wealth of apt quotation and charming reminiscence."

Tennyson on his walks would recite out loud to himself new passages and new lines for his poems which suddenly came to him; a habit, we are told, that had always been his since his boyhood. Colonel McCabe, from whom I have just quoted, has recorded that in reply to many of his questions as to the genesis of certain lines Tennyson always replied that they "came to him."

It was on High Down that Tennyson's poem The Charge of the Light Brigade "came to him" suddenly. The poem was printed as a fly-leaf and sent out to the Crimea, 1854, for the soldiers to read. "Break, break, break, on thy cold grey stones, O Sea !" also "came to him" in a moment. "Crossing the Bar" he wrote at the age of eighty in five minutes as he was going from Lymington to Yarmouth. His son tells us, in his Memoir of his Father, "that his best working days were in the early Spring, when nature begins to awaken from her winter sleep." We are told, too, about the Poet's "sacred pipes," one half-an-hour after breakfast, the other pipe half-an-hour after dinner, when no one was allowed to be with him, for it was then that his best thoughts came to him.

The Poet's summer-house in Maiden's Croft still stands as he built it. Here he wrote "Enoch Arden" as well as many others of his poems. Hallam Lord Tennyson has told me how his father would walk up and down the meadow in front of this summer-house on starlight nights and "lines and great thoughts would come to him."

Tennyson was devoted to the stars. It was Professor Tyndall who explained to my mother that the very special beauty of the stars at Freshwater is due to the fact that we are on a small Island and the water all round gives a remarkable luminosity and glory to the heavens above. On the roof at Farringford is a wooden platform which Tennyson had built on purpose that he might go out at night to look at the stars. William Allingham records in his Diary: "October; 4th, 1863. Tennyson takes me upstairs to his den on the top storey and higher up still to a ladder up to the leads. He often comes up here a-night to look at the heavens. One night he was watching shooting stars and tumbled through the hatchway, falling on the floor below, a height of at least ten feet, I should say. The ladder · probably broke his fall and he was not hurt. I quoted to him, 'A certain star shot madly from his sphere.' Tennyson, ' I've never heard any Sea Maids' Music in Freshwater Bay, but I saw an old lady swimming one day.' "

Hallam Lord Tennyson describes in his Memoir a dinner party at Swainston and his father saying he must leave the table to look at the Comet, and all the company followed the Poet out on to the lawn. "They saw Arcturus seemingly dance as if mad when it passed out of the Comet's tail, and Tennyson said, 'It is like a besom of destruction sweeping the sky.' Next night he observed 'the Comet from his own roof platform' " and when he came down his son tells us his father read some "Paradise Lost."

Tennyson's knowledge of astronomy was remarkable, and from the above source we read that "the accuracy of his talk about the stars surprised more than one of the great astronomers."

The Poet's knowledge of Botany was also very great. I remember a Cambridge Professor who challenged the Poet's statement that the daisies had crimson markings on their under petals. The criticiser came back from his walk on Tennyson Down discomfited — every daisy he picked was just as the Poet had stated it to be.

In "The Gardener's Daughter" Tennyson describes her hair

"more black than ash-buds in the front of March." There is an ash tree growing by the path under the Down which leads to Tennyson's Cross, which Hallam Lord Tennyson would point out to me as illustrating his father's line. It is interesting to go and look at this tree in early spring and see how amazingly black the buds are and what a wonderful description it is of a woman's hair. By this ash tree grows the thick hedge where "The blackthorn blossom fades and falls and leaves the bitter sloe." The yew tree of which Tennyson wrote in The Holy Grail, "O brother, I have seen this yew-tree smoke" you will see at Farringford; it grows opposite the morning room window. The smoke is the pollen which in spring is blown from the tree by the wind. Another mention of the "smoking yew" is in "In Memoriam." Close to the yew tree grows the Yucca of which he wrote "My Yucca which no winter quells" and which "pushed towards our faintest sun a spike of half-accomplished bells." The Hawthorns with their "pearls of May" grow along the entrance drive to Farringford. But one could go on for a very long time quoting lines in which he makes reference to birds, trees, and flowers.

Mrs. Margaret Woods, herself a poet, tells us that Tennyson coming upon a bed of forget-me-nots in his garden at Farringford exclaimed: "Heavens up-breaking through the earth!" This line he afterwards applied to the bluebells in his description of the spring ride of Guinevere and Lancelot to King Arthur's Court.

"February fair child" we all know, and to see the Farringford snowdrops in their glory, is a sight never to be forgotten.

His poem "The Flower," "Once in a golden hour I cast to earth a seed," was written from watching some Love in Idleness seeds, growing at Farringford.

Has any poet written more about birds than Tennyson? His old shepherd used to say that of an early morning when he went to look at his flock, "the birds all round the house (Farringford) would be singing like a charm."

"O birds that warble to the morning sky ....
O birds that warble as the day goes by"
seems to sum up all Freshwater in Spring time.

Maud was written at Farringford. The rocks still call Maud! Maud! Maud! while Hallam Lord Tennyson in his Memoir of his father, tells us "Maud is here, here, here," is like the call of the little birds.

"The Throstle" was written by Tennyson in his summer-house in the kitchen garden. The words are to illustrate the song of the thrush, who always repeats his notes twice over.

"O Blackbird ! sing me something well:
While all the neighbours shoot thee round,
I keep smooth plats of fruitful ground
Where thou mays't warble, eat, and dwell"

though not written at Farringford, might well have been, for the garden there holds true to the tradition of food and welcome and protection for all bird life.

I wish it could be said that all Tennyson's great poems about the sea had been written at Farringford, but we can claim "The Revenge," "Enoch Arden," and "Crossing the Bar."

The Poet used to say: "Listen to the sound of the sea in this line," and repeat "The League-long roller thundering on the reef" (Enoch Arden). Tennyson's line in "Maud" "Now to the scream of a madden'd beach dragg'd down by the wave" was denounced by the reviewers of

"Maud" as extravagant and exaggerated, and it is interesting to read what Professor Tyndall says of Freshwater Bay in a storm. "I sat near the shore observing the advance of the waves and listening to their thunder. The pebbles and shingles on the beach are mainly flint, and emit a sharp sound on collision with each other. As the billows break and roll up the beach they carry the shingle along with them, and on their retreat they drag it downwards. Here the collisions of the flint pebbles are innumerable. They blend together in a continuous sound which could not be better described than by the line in 'Maud.'"

"O did ye never lie upon the shore and watch the curl'd white of the coming wave glass'd in the slippery sand before it breaks."
(Merlin and Vivien.)

In these lines Hallam Lord Tennyson tells us "his father thought of Alum Bay, if anywhere."

In "Geraint and Enid" I always think that the dress which Earl Doorm offered Enid, is like our sea at Freshwater on a calm summer day.

"Where, like a shoaling sea, the lovely blue
Play'd into green."

In opposition to the peace of the sea, is the storm in "Sea Dreams": "The sea roars ruin: a fearful night!"

After Tennyson's death a poet wrote of his deep love and understanding of Nature:

"He look'd on Nature's lowest thing
For some sublime God's word:
And lived for ever listening
Lest God should speak unheard."

It is the honour and glory of Freshwater that on the tablet put up to his memory in our beautiful old church is the following inscription:

In loving memory
of
Alfred Lord Tennyson

Whose happiest days were passed
at Farringford in this Parish.

Born August 6th, 1809.
Died October 6th, 1892.

Buried in Westminster Abbey
October 12th, 1892.

G. F. WATTS, O.M., R.A.

" The soul of man is larger than the sky,
Deeper than ocean, or the abysmal dark
Of the unfathomed centre."

G. F. WATTS, O.M., R.A., AND THE BRIARY *

George Frederick Watts, painter, sculptor and prophet, was born in 1817 and died in 1904. It is good to think of his presence here at Freshwater, even though it was for so short a time.

G. F. Watts was not only the great artist, he was also a great thinker and teacher. He is quoted as saying "I paint ideas," and it was by the medium of his pictures that he gave his teaching to the world. It was the significance of life, more than life itself, that absorbed him. His symbolism will become more and more understood as the reality of the world of spirit around us is accepted. Watts taught in his noble pictures that he would have us live in the "Eternal Now" where all is controlled by Divine Law. With chance and fate he had no patience. Like the great mystic Jakob Boehme, he saw "with the eyes of the soul into the heart of things." His greatest lesson to us is "the reality of the power of love," which theme he has given us in a beautiful series of pictures of which the most famous are "Love Triumphant," "Love and Life," "Love and Death." The following words of Fenwick L. Holmes explain Watts's message to the world so clearly that it seems fit they should be quoted: "Dream your dreams, see your visions, picture your good, knowing that you draw forth from the inexhaustible resources of heaven just what your faith demands. Vision and faith will carry you across every sea of despair, every mountain of difficulty. Ask, with faith; believing."

Of Watts's consummate skill as a portrait painter his friend the Poet wrote –

* The Briary was destroyed by fire, March, 1934.

"As when a painter, poring on a face,
Divinely, thro' all hindrance, finds the man
Behind it, and so paints him that his face,
The shape and colour of a mind and life,
Lives for his children, ever at its best."

It has been well said that Watts painted *the mind* of the reign of Queen Victoria: statesmen, viceroys, soldiers, philosophers, painters, poets, musicians are all there, and, as Tennyson says, mind and life at its best is recorded for all time. A very celebrated Watts portrait is the one of Mrs. Nassau Senior, who lived at Warden Lodge, Colwell Bay; a picture of "splendid opulence and power" is the description of it by a well known art critic. Of Tennyson there are four or five magnificent portraits. One is at Farringford, there is also there the exquisite portrait of the Poet's wife, and the picture of his two sons.*

Of special interest to us who live at Freshwater are the two or three landscapes painted in this neighbourhood which are to be seen at the Watts Gallery, Compton. **

---

* *Both are now in the Usher Gallery Lincoln.*
** *Near Guildford, Surrey. (Ed. 1993)*

II

It is a lovely field path, shaded by spreading Elms, * that leads from Farringford to The Briary, which was built by Watts for his friends Mr. and Mrs. Prinsep. Philip Webb, the friend of William Morris, was architect. Three huge studios were built for the Painter, and are still there. The date of the house is 1873. It stands at the foot of Tennyson Down. Everything about The Briary is alluring — the smiling lawns and terraces, the clipped yew hedges, and the great magnolia tree which covers the front of the house, "a livelier emerald twinkles on the grass " than anywhere else, and the complete loveliness of the place takes hold of the strings of one's heart. The story of the house is as follows: Tennyson said to his friend the Painter, "Why not come and build a house down here ?" and Watts, who was looking for a house for his friends Mr. and Mrs. Prinsep, accepted the idea; the land was bought, the house built, and christened "The Briary" from the profusion of roses that grew on the banks of the drive that led up to the house. Two great cypress trees used to mark the entrance to this drive, and gave one a sense of Italy.

Round the front of the house one can still see the red brick path which Watts had specially made for Mr. Prinsep so that he could go out in all weathers. Mr. Prinsep when he came to The Briary was somewhat of an invalid. He was adored, and all the charming people fought to be allowed to read out loud to him.

I have heard from those who knew The Briary in these days how "full of noble thought and aspiration the house was," and tradition still speaks of the very remarkable set of people who lived there, and how much the influence of "Signor " (the name by which the Painter was known to his friends) contributed to the atmosphere of the house.

Alas all lost through the Dutch Elm disease in the 1970's (Ed 1993)

Signor and Mr. Prinsep wore cloaks and broad hats, and so did Tennyson and his brothers. People walking in the lanes would stop to watch them pass, and a visitor to Freshwater was heard pathetically exclaiming "Is there no one who is commonplace here? Is everybody either a poet, or a genius, or a painter, or peculiar in some way?"

Mrs. Watts in her "Annals of a Painter's Life" describes The Briary as seen from within, and says, "Old furniture and the household gods, brought from Little Holland House, which Mrs. Prinsep knew so well how to place, made the new house seem old. Mr. Prinsep, now an invalid, was the centre of solicitude. At luncheon Mrs. Prinsep sat at the head of the table and reigned over her large family party, looking like the wife of an Italian Doge transplanted into the nineteenth century, Mr. Prinsep seated beside her, and on his other side was the beautiful young widow, their niece, Mrs. Herbert Duckworth. Then Andrew Hichens and his lovely young wife, May,* not yet married a year; and her sister Annie Prinsep, my particular friend of all the party. And there was Signor with a child on each side, and this was the group I remember round that hospitable table."

In the Dictionary of National Biography we can read of Mr. Prinsep's eminence as an administrator in India, and later on of his distinguished career as a Member of Council at the India Office in London. You can also read in this same book an account of their son, the well known painter Val Prinsep, R.A., as well as of Mr. Prinsep's brother, Charles, who was also a very eminent Indian Civil Servant. He was the father of May Lady Tennyson and Annie Prinsep. How much Freshwater owes to May Lady Tennyson can only be told by

May was the niece and adopted daughter of Mr. and Mrs. Prinsep. Her second husband was Hallam Lord Tennyson. Her portrait by Watts was at Farringford; another of her by Watts is in the Compton Picture Gallery. She was buried at Compton and her brother and sister placed a plaque in her memory in All Saints, Freshwater. (Ed. 1993)

those who knew her. She died 19th July, 1931. Her sister, Annie Prinsep, still lives; and is a vital force of help and example to us all.*

Traditions of Watts at Freshwater are alas ! few. He appears in our annals as a rider rather than as an artist ! and there are many stories of him out riding every day on a beautiful Arab horse, and of expeditions to Swainston, with Tennyson leading the way in his own big carriage, while Watts followed on horseback. A farm on the way to Brook is pointed out as having been one of the favourite places where the friends liked to picnic. There are legends, too, of Watts playing the violin at Dimbola and of people in the road stopping to listen to the Painter's music floating over the hedge.

My mother writes of a visit to the Painter: "Watts was in his studio among his beautiful dreams. He looked more like Titian than ever. He gets up at four every morning and starts work, and he paints all the noble fancies which come into his mind. 'Better to wear out than rust out,' he said. I told him how I admired his picture of Joachim, and he said: 'I tried to put some music into it.' "

By permission of Mrs. Watts I am allowed to quote the following description of her husband and Tennyson, which she wrote for her own beautiful book, "The Annals of a Painter's Life" :

"Signor had been at work at Farringford while Miss Liddle and I had spent the morning together under a big elm on the Briary lawn, and when one o'clock came we went to meet the party, as Lord Tennyson and his son had arranged to walk back with Signor. We had just climbed the little rise that led to a broad green glade when the three came in sight, and we both exclaimed. For down the great aisle

Since these words were written Miss Prinsep has died. She passed away at Ryde on 29th December, 1932.

of elms there came a white Russian deer-hound flashing like silver through the sun and shade, and the central figure the Poet, a note of black in the midst of the vivid green, grand in the folds of his ample cloak, and his face looming grandly from the shadow of the giant hat. 'Monumental' Signor would have called him. Tennyson's slight stoop and the heavier step of age, made the youthful figure of his son look all the more what he was, his father's vigorous staff and prop. And then our eyes fell on the delicate grey figure of our beloved Painter on the other side, the grey hat crowning silver hair, a grey cloak taking pleasant folds while he stepped like a boy, light and neat in every movement. Lord Tennyson was playful, gave us a smiling greeting, and put out the crook of his walking stick for us to shake hands with.

"As we went towards The Briary the teeming life of nature seemed to turn their thoughts to a life beyond this life. Lord Tennyson quoted with regret the saddest epitaph he knew, written by a friend who had no belief in the future; and then with moistening eyes he gave us the triumphant words placed over a woman's grave: 'I have loved, I love, I shall love.' But given in the terse Latin, 'Amavi, Amo, Amabo.' "

MRS. CAMERON AND DIMBOLA

Dimbola * (now the Dimbola Hotel), with its smiling bay windows and low picturesque gables, stands halfway between Farringford and the sea. The house is sun-drenched, and its romantic view of the sea and rocks made it indeed a fit home for Mrs. Cameron, who loved everything that was beautiful.

It was here that she lived, ruled, and devoted her life to art, to friendship, and to being kind to everybody. Her dynamic and all-compelling individuality, her unconventionality, and her outspoken frankness were the delight as well as the astonishment of her hosts of friends.

She is famous for her pioneer work in photography. Before her marriage she was one of the well known Miss Pattles, one of whom became Mrs. Prinsep and was celebrated for her salon at Little Holland House; ** another, Countess Somers, who was renowned for her beauty; another, Lady Dalrymple, who was beloved for her kindness, each one of the seven sisters being remarkable in a different way. Mrs. Cameron was born at Calcutta in 1815 and died in Ceylon in 1879. In middle age she took up photography and settled at Freshwater in 1860.

In a book, long since out of print, my mother says: "It is almost

---

* *It was later divided into two and now the first half, renamed Cameron House has been saved by The Cameron House Trust to become a living and working museum for the benefit of Islanders and tourists alike. (Ed. 1993)*
** *It was after Little Holland House that Mr. and Mrs. Prinsep came to Freshwater.*

MRS. JULIA MARGARET CAMERON

There is no great and no small
>   To the Soul that maketh all;
And where it cometh, all things are;
>   And it cometh everywhere.

impossible to describe Mrs. Cameron; she played the game of life with such vivid courage and disregard for ordinary rules: she entered into other people's interests with such warm-hearted sympathy and determined devotion, that though her subjects may have occasionally rebelled, they generally ended by gratefully succumbing to her rule, laughing and protesting all the time."

How Mrs. Cameron came to live at Dimbola is told by my mother, in this same book, and she writes: "I have heard Mrs. Cameron describe how it was during a short visit to Farringford that one day, on a sudden impulse, she agreed to purchase a couple of houses by the roadside from a certain Jacob Long, an old sailor, who sailed the high seas and dabbled in bricks and mortar when on shore. Jacob Long's houses were purchased and furnished, and planted with ivy and sweet briar and christened "Dimbola," after one of the Cameron estates in Ceylon, for Mr. Cameron had amassed a considerable fortune while in India which he had invested in coffee estates in Ceylon."

It was at Dimbola that Mrs. Cameron first began to photograph, and in her "Annals of a Glass House" she says: "I turned my coal house into a dark-room, and a glazed fowl house, which I had given to my children, became my glass house, and the society of hens and chickens was soon changed into that of poets, prophets, painters, and lovely maidens. I worked fruitlessly, but not hopelessly. I longed to arrest all the beauty that came across my way." *

Mrs. Cameron worked in the days when art in connection with the camera had never been thought of. She brought all her genius and energy to the development of her ideas. Anyone who has ever seen a "Daguerreotype" will realise the revolution Mrs. Cameron created

* *This Studio of Mrs. Cameron's was pulled down a few years ago.*
It stood on the lawn close to where the conservatory now is.

by her photographs. She held frequent exhibitions of her work at Colnagi's Gallery in London. Her portraits of famous people and her pictures of sacred subjects after the manner of the Italian masters revealed to an amazed public the possibilities of the camera. She gained gold, silver, and bronze medals in England, America, Austria, and Germany.

Her pictures of all the famous people who congregated round Tennyson at Farringford, form an historical record of very great interest and importance. The debt we owe to Mrs. Cameron for these portraits has never been sufficiently acknowledged, until the other day, when Mr. and Mrs. Perrin built the Perrin Gallery at Leighton House, Kensington, London, in which to exhibit permanently a collection of her work. These photographs include portrait studies of Carlyle, Tennyson, Ruskin, Tyndall, Darwin, Lord Dufferin, Palgrave, Sir Henry Taylor, Holman Hunt, Lecky, Sir John Herschel (the astronomer), Longfellow, Robert Browning, and Watts.

I have before me as I write an album of Mrs. Cameron's photographs which she made and gave to my mother. It is bound in dark green morocco and on the cover is printed, in letters of gold —

> Given to Annie Thackeray
> by her friend
> Julia Margaret Cameron
> Freshwater Bay, Isle of Wight.

On opening the album the first thing one sees is the following caution, written by Mrs. Cameron in her big bold handwriting: "*Fatal* to photographs are cups of tea and coffee, candles and lamps, and children's fingers!"

The beautiful book contains a very complete collection of Mrs. Cameron's experiments and achievements in photographic art. Under the first photograph Mrs. Cameron has written "The Madonna Aspentate," the composition and feeling reminding one of Raphael. Then comes another Holy Mother and Child, "La Madonna Riposata," for each picture is named by Mrs. Cameron. Then a very beautiful study of the head of her niece, Mrs. Herbert Duckworth, so beautiful that one feels photography never will or can go further. "The Three Marys at the Sepulchre" is full of poetry. It is followed by more Madonnas, after which there is a noble portrait study of G. F. Watts in the manner of Titian. An old wrinkled woman and a young child illustrate "Seventy years ago, my darling, seventy years ago" — which reminds me of Mrs. Cameron's saying that "No woman should ever allow herself to be photographed between the ages of eighteen and eighty." Then the representation of a young mother and her child, which is entitled "Goodness," but is not successful, as the sitters both look so terribly self-conscious. On the next page of the book is a picture under which Mrs. Cameron has written "A Sybil, after the manner of Michael Angelo," which is followed by the "Five Wise Virgins and the Five Foolish Virgins." Then a superb study of a woman's head called "St. Agnes," the draperies and lighting a masterpiece of photographic pictorial art. "The Salutation," after the manner of Giotto, is striking. Now comes a very beautiful woman's head entitled "A Dream," under which Mr. Watts has written "Quite divine." The well known portrait of Carlyle is included in the Album; of this, he wrote to Mrs. Cameron: "It is as if suddenly the picture began to speak, terrifically ugly and woe-begone, but has something of a likeness: my candid opinion."

Darwin has written under his portrait: "I like this photograph very much better than any other which has been taken of me. Charles Darwin."

Mrs. Cameron also photographed "Alice in Wonderland," who came with her sisters and her father, Dean Liddle, to stay at Freshwater one summer.

"Indeed," writes my mother, "Mrs. Cameron followed her art with extraordinary trouble and devotion, and also expected much from her sitters. Sitting to her was a serious affair, not to be lightly entered upon. Her sitters came at her summons, they trembled, or would have trembled, could they have dared, when the round black eye of the camera was turned upon them. They felt what consequences, what disastrous waste of time and money and effort might ensue from any passing quiver of emotion." For in those days Mrs. Cameron had to make her own plates, and her sitters would have to sit without moving for ten minutes while the cap was off the lens."

From her window Mrs. Cameron would keep an eye on the passers-by making their way down to the shore, and if they were good-looking she would send one of her maids running after them to beg them to come and sit to her.

This was the time when Mrs. Cameron was illustrating Tennyson's "Idylls of the King" and many sitters were needed, and I have heard descriptions of all the dressing up that was needed and of "strangely robed men and maidens issuing forth from the Glass House" where the photographs were taken.

Mr. Wilfred Ward has written: "Freshwater in these days seethed with intellectual life. The Poet was, of course, the centre, and that remarkable woman, Mrs. Cameron, was stage manager of what was, for us young people, a great drama. For Tennyson was still writing the "Idylls of the King" which had so greatly moved the whole country, and we felt that we were in the making of history . .

.. I recall her bringing Tennyson to my father's house, while she was photographing representatives for the characters, and calling out directly she saw Cardinal Vaughan (to whom she was a perfect stranger): "Alfred, I have found Sir Lancelot." Tennyson's reply was: "I want a face well worn with evil passion."

Tradition in Freshwater still tells of all the kindness and help given by Mrs. Cameron to people in trouble, and how all were made welcome to her house. I have heard my mother describe how her garden gate was never shut and how brown paper parcels were spread out on the lawn, as well as open pans of collodium which were used for developing the photographs. From my mother's descriptions I seem still to hear the echo of Mrs. Cameron's voice calling to her maids, and the voice of the master of the house reciting Homer aloud in the drawing room. Tennyson's description of him was "a philosopher with his beard dipped in moonlight."

The stories of Mrs. Cameron are legion. She planted a wild briar hedge, and when a friend remonstrated that the passers-by were picking her sweet briar and that there would soon be none left, she answered: "But that is why I planted it so that it should be picked and enjoyed." The same altruistic impulse made her grow each year primroses on the bank which separated her house from the main road down to the sea. She built the tower so that Dimbola might look beautiful to her friends as they walked up from the shore. For the sake of beauty no effort would be spared, a cabbage field at the back of the house was turned into a lawn in an incredibly short space of time, in order that an expected visitor should enjoy walks under the trees on soft down turf. One of the Bay windows she had built in twenty-four hours, so that her friend Sir Henry Taylor, on arriving to stay, might find the afternoon sunshine pouring in through his bed-room window.

A friend has told me how she was taken by Mrs. Cameron into Mr. Cameron's bed-room where he lay fast asleep on his bed. Mrs. Cameron, pointing to him, said: "Behold the most beautiful old man on earth." I recall the story of when Garibaldi came to Farringford to see Tennyson. Mrs. Cameron went down on her knees before him to implore him to sit for his photograph. Garibaldi did not understand this, and thought she was a beggar asking for alms.

Mrs. Cameron photographed all day long, and at night she would organise impromptu plays and dances in the big panelled hall, and partners would come out on to the lawn and dance under the stars. One warm, moonlight night the whole company, my mother describes, went streaming away across the fields up on to the Down. On another occasion Mrs. Cameron led her guests to Farringford, striking matches as she went to light the way. On stormy nights Tennyson would come to Dimbola to fetch Mrs. Cameron and they would go down to the shore together. Visitors to Dimbola should notice the green door leading into the lane at the back of the house through which Tennyson would always come. He hated to be looked at, and through this door he could avoid the publicity of the road down to the Bay.

Of a dinner party for Alfred Tennyson, Sir Henry Taylor, my mother, and the Misses Prinsep, at Dimbola, Mrs. Cameron writes: "We dined at seven and only got up from table at eleven o'clock. All the while the most brilliant conversation. The whole range of poetry, comprising every immortal poet brought to life and living again in the glowing wise breath of Alfred Tennyson and the quotations from Henry Taylor's rich and faithful memory.... They were like two brilliant fencers crossing their rapiers or flashing their foils, both giving and evading clean thrusts."

It was in 1860 that Darwin came with his family to Freshwater, and it was then that his photograph was taken. When Darwin wrote to Mrs. Cameron approving of the portrait he said "There are sixteen people in my house and every one your friend." The Darwins stayed at Redoubt House, next door to Dimbola, for the summer. Darwin brought his horse with him. Darwin's daughter told me the story of the horse and how her father rode up on to Afton Down the first morning and let the reins drop to see what his steed would do. The horse paused for a moment and then went straight off in the direction of Down, Darwin's home, from whence they had all come.

Redoubt House can boast of another famous guest, Jenny Lind, "The Swedish Nightingale," the most famous of prima donnas. Musicians will be interested to know that at Farringford is the little upright piano * on which the singer accompanied herself when she sang to Tennyson.

The house next to Redoubt was built for Tennyson's brother Frederick. Many interesting people have in turn stayed here. Dean Bradley, the famous Dean of Westminster, Leslie Stephen the critic, his sister the mystic, Lady Ritchie the writer. The house was christened Pannells by Hallam Lord Tennyson. In the old charters of the Farringford estate, as far back as the twelfth century, the land on which the house stands was known as "Pannells," which means a small patch of ground. All the Farringford fields have picturesque old names — "Maidens Croft," where Tennyson built his summer-house, was so called by the monks at Farringford after the Virgin Mary. Then there is "Friars' Pit," which one passes on the way up to Tennyson Down, where a Hermit dwelt; and "St. George," where the Archers shot, and "Clerks' Hill," where the Clerk of the Monastery lived.

* *Now at the Tennyson Research Centre, Central Library Lincoln (Ed. 1993)*

The "Terrace House" with the handsome iron gates at the end of the road is the property of the Tennyson family, and is interesting for its garden and its most beautiful views of the English Channel and the remembrance that Jowett of Oxford fame came here Spring after Spring to be near his friend the Poet.

On the left hand from the Dimbola Hotel stands "Hazlehurst," * under whose hospitable roof so many celebrities have stayed. Mrs. Calloway's** memories go back to Tennyson and Mrs. Cameron, for whom she often posed for camera pictures. Her interesting talk should not be missed by anyone who wishes to obtain information about the great men and women of the Victorian age at Freshwater.

Next door to Mrs. Calloway's house is "The Porch," a little cottage which, when built by Mrs. Cameron, stood in the fields. It was christened "The Porch" by Mrs. Cameron after the celebrated Athenian Porch where Socrates and Plato held forth to admiring crowds. Jowett was at this time translating Plato, and Mrs. Cameron built "The Porch" for him, in which to work and stay. The appearance of the cottage has been altered since the creepers were pulled down and the Porch itself taken away. It was here that my mother came constantly to stay before her marriage, and here for many years we spent happy holidays, and during the war made the cottage our home.

Beach House (now the Afton Down Hotel) must be mentioned.*** It was here that Lord Bryce would come, and Miss Prinsep has sent me a letter from William Allingham in which he writes to his friend Madame de la Tour "It is highly interesting to hear of John Milton's descendants in Beach House, especially as my friend Mrs. Tennant and her daughters, living under the same roof, are lineal descendants of Oliver Cromwell."

On the opposite side of the road in The Square.
**Mrs. Calloway died March, 1936.*
***Flats opposite The Albion Hotel. (Ed. 1993)*

A daughter of Dean Allen, the close friend of Tennyson, wrote to me the other day about the Past and said "Great men are sent into the world 'to help us on our way,' " and now let me end this little book with a word of loving gratitude to all the dear and noble people who knew and loved Freshwater. As Sir Henry Taylor writes:

" . . . . such souls,
Whose sudden visitations daze the world,
Vanish like lightning, but leave behind
A voice that in the distance far away
Wakens the slumbering ages."

APPENDIX

A LIST OF SOME OF THE FAMOUS PEOPLE WHO HAVE STAYED AT FRESHWATER

PAINTERS
Holman Hunt, O.M., R.A.
Sir John Millais, Bt., P.R.A.
Frederick Walker, R.A.
Edward Lear.
George Du Maurier.
Briton Riviere, R.A.
Mrs. Allingham.
Kate Greenaway.

POETS
Longfellow.
Oliver Wendell Holmes.
Lowell.
Sir Henry Taylor, K.C.M.G.
Aubrey de Vere.
William Allingham.
Mrs. Brotherton.
Mrs. Margaret Woods.

MEN OF SCIENCE
Darwin.
Professor Owen.
Professor Tyndall.
Sir William Herschel
    (the Astronomer).

WRITERS
Edward Fitz Gerald.
Professor Jowett,
    Master of Balliol.
Sir Alfred Lyall, G.C.B.
Lord Bryce.
Leslie Stephen.
Bayard Taylor.
Sir Herbert Warren.
Sir Richard Jebb.
Henry Butcher.
Wilfred Ward.
The Honourable Arthur Elliot.
W. G. Ward.
D. W. Freshfield.
Anne Thackeray Ritchie.
Virginia Woolf.
Desmond MacCarthy.

MUSICIANS
Sir Hubert Parry.
Sir Charles Stanford.
Jenny Lind.

CHURCHMEN
Archbishop Temple.
Archbishop Benson.
Philip Brooks.
F. D. Maurice.
Dean Bradley,
    Dean of Westminster.

SOME BOOKS TO READ AT FRESHWATER

Tennyson. A Memoir by Hallam Lord Tennyson.
Tennyson and His Friends. Edited by Hallam Lord Tennyson.
The Diary of William Allingham. Edited by Mrs. Allingham
Annals of a Painter's Life. By his wife, Mary Watts.
Tennyson, Browning, and Ruskin. By Anne Thackeray Ritchie.
From Friend to Friend. By Anne Thackeray Ritchie.
The Memoirs of Lady Troubridge.

Other Hunnyhill Publications

The Wordsworth Poetical Guide to the Lakes
Richard J. Hutchings

West Country Poems of Wordsworth and Coleridge
Richard J. Hutchings

A Gentleman's Tour, 1776
Elizabeth Hutchings

Discovering the Sculptures of G.F. Watts, O.M., R.A.
Elizabeth Hutchings

From An Island
Anne Thackeray Ritchie
(Foreword by Belinda Norman-Butler)

Further Reading

The Farringford Journal of Emily Tennyson   1853 - 1864
Richard J. Hutchings and Dr. Brian Hinton   1986

Alfred and Emily Tennyson – A Marriage of True Minds
Richard J. Hutchings   1991
Published by the Isle of Wight County Press

Immortal Faces – Julia Margaret Cameron in the Isle of Wight
Dr. Brian Hinton   1992
Published by The Isle of Wight County Press and the Isle of Wight County Council

Idylls of Farringford
Richard J. Hutchings

Dickens on an Island
Richard J. Hutchings

Distributed by Hunnyhill Publications